I0116199

Common Sense 2026

© 2025 by Jack Forge

First softcover edition: January 2026

Published independently in the United States of America

Cover and interior design by Jack Forge

Plow illustration: public domain, 19th-century engraving

ISBN-13: 979-8-9940669-0-4 (hardcover)

ISBN-13: 979-8-9940669-1-1 (paperback)

ISBN-13: 979-8-9940669-2-8 (ebook)

Printed in the United States of America

10 9 8 7 6 5 4 3 2 1

The first edition, with appendix.

"Society in every state is a blessing, but government even in its best state is but a necessary evil…"

- PAINE.

UNITED STATES

January 10, 2026.

MMXXVI

COMMON SENSE

By Jack R. Forge

"You are not the victim of the system, you are its architect."

Jack R. Forge

INTRODUCTION:
Of The Present State of American Affairs in 2026.

Two and a half centuries ago, on January 10, 1776, Thomas Paine's *Common Sense* was published. Several months later, on July 4th, 1776, the United States was born when the thirteen original colonies declared independence from Great Britain. On July 4th, 2026, the United States will be 250 years old.

When *Common Sense* was first published, Thomas Paine was advocating for independence from foreign rule. Today, we no longer need independence from a foreign power — we need independence from an internal threat to democracy. That new threat is the algorithm. The new parliament is the outrage cycle.

This is not an attack on you, the individual. It is not an indictment of character or values. You are not broken; your behavior has been weaponized against your own interests. There is a difference. You are capable of self-governance; you may have been convinced to outsource it. The individual is not the problem, abdication is.

That internal threat is the intentional destabilization of the United States, disguised as patriotism. The United States articulated principles of truth, justice, and human dignity that resonated throughout the world - even when America itself failed to live them. It does not live in the agenda of the left or the right. It stands on its principles — to protect its people. We can and should disagree civilly on what that means, for disagreement, done in good faith, is how a free nation strengthens itself.

The American Revolution articulated the ideals of human dignity, self-governance, and basic rights. Those principles have inspired people around the world and empowered excluded groups within this country to fight for inclusion.

The poisoning we face today comes from those who wrap themselves in the cloak of patriotic language while actively undermining those foundational ideals — whether through disinformation, authoritarianism, or tribal loyalty at the expense of principle.

Examples of this chosen neglect, which often arise from both sides of the political aisle, can be found in the use of the phrase "threat to democracy." Both Republicans and Democrats have challenged elections. Democrats challenged the election of George W. Bush. Donald Trump challenged the election of Joe Biden. Both challenges—regardless of the reader's opinion—were made within the confines of democracy. They were legal and within the rights of each party to pursue. The actual threat to democracy was not the legal challenge itself, but the destabilizing rhetoric used by both sides. Legal challenges within the agreed-upon rules by both sides are fine. Riots, lies, and loyalty oaths to losing candidates are not.

I am not claiming to agree with either challenge. The point is not *who* was right, but *how* we describe those actions. If we believe our side is justified while condemning the other for the same act, *we* are the problem—the other side of the same coin.

Another example of this deeper fracturing of democracy is the "othering" of our political opponents. They are not our enemies; they are our fellow citizens. When both Democrats and Republicans label their opponents as a "threat to democracy," the real threat is not the opponent—it is the act of othering itself. If both sides say the other is a threat to democracy, who is actually threatening whom?

People celebrated and mocked the death of a man in the public square, all because he was trying to have a conversation with those who disagreed with him. That is destabilizing.

Political division that leads to the refusal to compromise, driven by the belief that the "other" is an existential threat, is what endangers democracy most.

When we cannot see that we're guilty of what we accuse others of doing, we've lost the capacity for self-examination that self-governance requires. And without that capacity, we become exactly what we fear - a people incapable of governing themselves.

The founders of the United States did not get everything right. They were imperfect in their perfection. Yet, they were wise enough to design a system that could grow and adapt with the times. The United States is not great because it is perfect — it is great because it can change, learn, and strive to be better.

The founders' belief that governments derive legitimacy from the consent of the governed, and that certain rights are inherent to human beings, remains revolutionary and right. Their failures to live up to those principles do not diminish the power of the ideas themselves. It was those very principles that gave the disenfranchised, the enslaved, and women the moral foundation to demand inclusion.

America's greatness is not its flawlessness. Its greatness lies in its ability to self-correct — to expand the meaning of "We the People."

A perfect citizen is one who does not expect a perfect government — and who does not expect that government to solve all of their problems.

CHAPTER 1

Of Self-Governance and the Abdication Thereof.

Self-governance is not voting every four years, then complaining about the results. It is not blaming others, sowing distrust, or believing things that are not true. Self-governance is personal responsibility; it is not taking everything we hear as truth and dispelling anything uncomfortable as untrue. Self-governance is being honest with ourselves, regardless of political affiliation. It is seeking out the full story, not just living in an echo chamber. We are not the victims of our choices. We are their creators.

The constitution does not govern us; we govern ourselves through it. The constitution is a broad framework from which we govern and guide ourselves. It is not a leash, it is a plow. We have to be the ones who pull it. We have collectively accepted this document as the guiding foundational piece to our democracy. We have accepted that this document is the way to govern ourselves through its principles. The founders clearly did not create this form of government for passive subjects. Thomas Paine himself challenged this through his original *Common Sense*. The founders set up a form of government for the people, driven by the people, not a king or a nanny. It is when we become spectators, not participants that the public rots.

We have voted for liars we know will lie, then cling to "our side" in fear of the "other" that we have been told to fear. However, we know the other, it is our neighbor we have dinner with, sit at the bar and drink with, those we work with, and there is nothing to fear. Yet, we feed ourselves with this new tyranny of misinformation for decades.

It is when we become spectators of government, not participants in government is when problems arise. Yet we continue to vote for "our side" in fear of the "other side" because of the political othering that has gone on for too long.

We as individuals need to stop enabling behavior. Enabling harmful behavior under the guise of being helpful or kind, at a minimum, is naïve; at worst, purposeful manipulation to subjugate those less fortunate. Learned helplessness is a problem, entitlement is a problem, and comfort becomes a prison that we allow ourselves to hide under while we blame others. Learned helplessness turns capable people into dependents. Self-governance means we as individuals stop enabling others in order to perform patriotism, to say we are good, to say we are helpful. We do not need a government program to take from us and give to the poor. We can do it ourselves. This is not about dismantling social safety nets; it is about empowerment. A value is not something we say we have; it is something we live by.

If we demand that the elected lawmakers act on our behalf and fire them through the election process if they don't, we take our power back. I was sitting in a meeting once with a politician who was discussing a political issue. This politician made the comment that there was nothing that could be done about it (referring to political gridlock). That is a politician who needed to be fired. They were the only ones in the room that day given the elected power to do something. They chose learned helplessness.

Your neighbor is not the enemy. Not looking in the mirror is. Blaming others and externalizing the problem is. It is when we excuse the abuse of power if it wears our colors. We need to stop dismissing lies, riots, and oaths of loyalty if they fit "our" narrative. The new taxation without representation has become hypocrisy.

Thomas Paine spoke out against the King; the new king to speak out against is the algorithm. This distracts you even when you know what you are hearing and seeing is not true; it is a distraction disguised as truth. It takes profits from your rage and divides us all. Your feed is not the town square; it is based on tailored interests to subjugate you further. It is a coliseum where you are merely entertained. You have been subjugated by your new king, the algorithm.

The things we entertain are the things that lead us down the path we are on. Every swipe is a vote for the new king.

However, we need to stop looking for the government to solve our problems. We need to stop looking for regulation to handle everything.

We have a choice: we can continue to feel good about performative acts, or we can actively live out our values. We need to stop dismissing abuse of power and abuse in general if it is on "our" side, and condemn the other side.

Stop waiting for the government to save you. Start governing yourself –
today. Or admit you prefer chains.

The Plow sits in the field. Who will pull it?

CHAPTER II.

How We've Dropped the Plow.

If I trust the truth, it is more accurate to the human experience than it is to a political ideology. It is closer to our core values than any party slogan.

You cannot help an individual by telling them there is no danger on the road they walk. Telling someone they're succeeding when they are failing may be kindness that buries them. Real help requires honest assessment.

We have been trained to believe systemic issues are wisdom, and focusing on the individual as too simple or naïve. I believe that is backwards. We have been sold the idea that systemic understanding is profound insight. But what if it's just a sophisticated way to surrender to the powers that be? That surrender is part of the cost of abdication. We have been trained by the system to blame structures for every problem. We are sold that systems are the bogeyman, and have given them more power than they deserve. If we wait for perfect conditions, we guarantee our own powerlessness. This is not about denying real barriers; it is about refusing to let the barriers own us. The plow waits for no one.

We don't live in the ideal world; we live in the world to try to make it ideal.

Throughout history, societies that tried to equalize outcomes rather than opportunities found themselves with less of both. Not because the idea wasn't compassionate, but because it misunderstood human nature. People need to see the connection between effort and reward. Remove that connection - whether through excessive government control or through inherited wealth that requires no effort - and you get the same result: entitlement, resentment, and decline.

The American experiment was revolutionary because it said: we won't guarantee equal outcomes, but we'll protect equal opportunity to pursue them. The founders did not guarantee a trophy. They guaranteed you have a shot.

Societies can't thrive through collective self-deception. Policies that feel compassionate but contradict human nature will fail. Facing reality - however uncomfortable - is the only path to sustainable governance. Policies that feel good (everyone gets equal outcomes, no one fails, everything is fair) but contradict human psychology and observable reality will fail - not because of political ideology, but because they're built on comfortable lies rather than uncomfortable truths.

We reward the most extreme voices with our attention, our clicks, and our outrage. We engage with content that makes us angry because it feels good to feel righteous. We've trained the algorithm - and ourselves - to amplify instability. We could scroll past, disengage, and demand better. Instead, we feed the beast and then complain we're being eaten by it. We are not the victims of the feed; we created it.

The lie we tell ourselves is an emotional one, not a logical one. We will vote for what feels good, even when the truth tells us it is not true. We crave the warm coat of "someone else will fix it." Some want government handouts, some want corporate trickle-down. Aren't both pacifiers? They both scream, "I won't govern myself."

Everyone has the opportunity to start a business, take risks, succeed, or fail. Rewarding those who take risks and create jobs is not the same as the government creating dependency. The difference is: one system is based on voluntary exchange and individual initiative, the other on forced redistribution.

We've become a nation of people who want someone else to solve our problems. Some of us want the government to do it through programs and redistribution. Others want corporations and markets to do it through trickle-down benefits. But both impulses reflect the same abdication: we've stopped believing we can solve problems through direct action in our own communities. We vote for people who promise to take care of us, whether through government checks or corporate jobs, rather than taking responsibility for building resilient local communities ourselves.

Self-governance means exactly that - governing the *self*. When I worked in residential treatment, I told the boys: This place works when everyone worries about themselves and chooses the rules, not because of force. Success came when they saw the benefit of mutual cooperation. The moment they waited for me to make them behave, or blamed each other for the program's problems, everything broke down. A nation is no different. Law without self-control is chains without locks.

We have politicians openly and blatantly stating they will not enforce laws they do not like. We have politicians undermining public trust by telling their constituents not to follow the law. This is intentional destabilization of society in the name of ideology.

Defund the police is the loudest treason in saint's clothing. It is not reform, it is the abolition of social structure. When cities burned in 2020, the mob did not say mend the plow; they cried Burn it down. Crime did not stop; it swallowed the poor and those in need of help. Neighborhoods destroyed, local shops lost, economic opportunities gone, and trauma increased the harm to those who need help. That is not compassion! A nation without order is no nation at all. The other side of the coin is defending institutions that intend to do good, while we tolerate the wolf in sheep's clothing. Abuse is abuse whether it is done by the badge, the priest, the politician, or the citizen. Blind loyalty to any idol or slogan is poison. Both sides swing the axe at the same plow. Who will pull the plow when it lies in pieces?

The politician does not take the social worker for security; why should you? Believe what they do, not what they say. Abuse is abuse, no matter what you want to call it. People who break the law purposefully are responsible for their behavior, the consequences; they are not victims of society. Crime is not synonymous with poverty.

Some lives are derailed by bad systems or luck; many others by the choices they make. We can show compassion for the former, and should not invent excuses for the latter. A teenager who steals out of hunger deserves a different response than a teenager who steals because he wants an electronic he can't afford. The first may be a victim of circumstance, and the second is a criminal who is victimizing others. Confusion between the two does not help the hungry, and it enables the criminal to continue the cycle and harm others. Justice and compassion in their truest form require telling the truth about both.

To blame the system is destabilizing, whether intentional or out of naiveté. It still serves the same purpose. That does not mean we should ignore social patterns; it just suggests again that we take personal responsibility for our actions. If we all demand ourselves to follow our values, then the system changes. It does not change when we all externalize the blame.

There was a business that used the idea of a meeting as a way to solve its problems. They would have them weekly. Once at the meeting, they spent their time discussing the problem, then, at the end of the meeting, they solved nothing, and scheduled another meeting to solve the problem. What they did not understand was that the meeting itself did not solve the problem; they actually had to have solutions, that they had to take into account for the problems, change, and do something about them. Crying, we have a problem, and blaming someone else never solves the problem. Legislating solutions for problems legislation created is destabilizing.

We can have all the right structures, all the right laws, all the right institutions - but if citizens are waiting to be governed rather than governing themselves, if we're blaming each other rather than examining our own behavior, the whole thing falls apart.

We've become a nation of people waiting for someone else to fix things. Some want the government to do it. Others want the market to do it. But both are forms of abdication - waiting for an external force to solve problems we should be addressing through our own choices and our own communities. The left says the government will save the poor, and the right wants the market to do so. Both say "I don't have to" at the individual level. We all can help others, individually, in our own communities. If we understand, both are necessary, but both need our help with honest assessment and accountability for one's own behavior.

Over recent decades, people across the political spectrum have been told to fear one another—to believe that compromise is weakness and that the "other side" cannot be trusted. Most citizens, liberal or conservative, do not actually live in such extremes. Yet our culture now amplifies the most unstable and polarizing voices, giving fringe opinions mainstream attention. What was once dismissed as the margin has become the message. The fringe now rules the stage, when it used to be dismissed as such, the fringe. The fringe has become mainstream poison.

The United States was founded on individuality and freedom from concentrated power. Any system—whether socialist, authoritarian, or corporatist—that centralizes power at the expense of the individual erodes that foundation. Centralized power is an old tyranny dressed in new clothing. Socialist by edict, corporatist by monopoly, and authoritarian by decree or force. All erode the individual. While the ideal of "equality for all" sounds noble, equality cannot be achieved by forcibly taking from some to give to others. True fairness lies not in guaranteed outcomes but in equal opportunity—the ability to know where one stands, to make changes, and to pursue one's own version of success. That is true equality. Equality of opportunity is the only thing fair that leaves the soul intact.

Societies must, of course, care for those in need. Safety nets should be a bridge, not a trap. But when such systems shift from empowerment to entitlement, they begin to harm those they were meant to help. Compassion that abuses is cruelty dressed in the saint's clothing. Learned helplessness can become institutionalized, breeding dependency rather than resilience. Compassion must never come at the cost of capability.

We have often, without realizing it, agreed to accept harm if it makes us feel good. Take taxation: we are taxed when we earn, spend, sell, and even when we die. And yet, we continue to tolerate inefficiency and waste as though it were inevitable. Government waste has become a national punchline, but it should instead be a national alarm. Waste is not inevitable. It should not be tolerated.

It is not honest to claim we love our neighbors while outsourcing that love to the bureaucrats we will never meet. We vote for things we deem generous without ever really understanding what we are voting for. There are strings attached that we do not see. That's not charity - that's performance. Real values require personal action, not proxy votes. Government relief is a crutch, not a virtue. If you would be free, govern your own generosity—or admit you prefer the chains of compulsion.

Self-governance, the individual who is not honest, waves a flag of patriotism; a true patriot pulls the plow. Call out your side, the waste and the lies, be honest with yourself, do an honest assessment of whether or not you say you have values, or if you live those values. Challenge yourself to read something you disagree with, listen to someone with an opposing view, and donate time or talent without demanding others do. Own yourself and your own behaviors.

The plow sits in the field. Who will pull it?

CHAPTER III.

The Present Cost of not Pulling.

When we fail to self-govern, when we abdicate our responsibility, is when we fail as a society. Throughout our history, Americans have unified through adversity - the Revolution, the Civil War (eventually), World Wars, and 9/11. Shared challenges forced us to see each other as fellow citizens rather than enemies.

But we've lost this capacity.

Today, even facing genuine threats - pandemics, economic crises, natural disasters - we fracture along tribal lines. We're so busy blaming each other that we can't address the actual problem. This is what abdication costs us: the ability to recognize common cause and act collectively when it matters most. It should not be that the left blames the right, and the right blames the left. The real enemy laughs.

The cost of abdicating our responsibility has led to people being told they cannot compromise, that they have to distance themselves from those who disagree with them. This has led to families fracturing, relationships ending, and violence. The cost is heavy, as it leads to harm to all of us. It is not acceptable to block streets, destroy cities, and police precincts because we do not like an outcome. Violence is not justified, and words are not violence. The cost comes at the expense of free speech being blamed. Free speech is not free from consequence; it means we are free to make the statement. Changing words to fit narratives, denying medical truths for political purposes, labeling every challenge as hateful or racist, especially when used to avoid an honest debate, is intellectually dishonest and manipulation designed to suppress free speech.

If we continue to allow abuse disguised as caring and compassion to continue, it creates within us a destabilization, personally, locally, and nationally. The cost is people openly celebrating harm to others, mocking the death of our opponents, and justifying abuse. People cheered the death of a man in the public square simply because he wanted to have a conversation. That is not who we are.

The cost is that, in the name of acceptance, institutions can drift into becoming indoctrination centers, diminishing freedom of thought and expression. We should celebrate being challenged. We should celebrate differences of opinion and be free to challenge others. The cost is someone's feelings of being offended, which has become more important than thought or freedom. When one is offended, it is their feelings; we are not responsible for how people feel, and we are responsible for how we treat them.

Classrooms used to be used to sharpen one's mind. Now they blunt the mind. We used to know that growth came through adversity; now we seek comfort and accept it, even though it imprisons us. Feelings have trumped facts, not for all, but for many. This is not acceptable; it is destabilizing. We should reject indoctrination, even if we favor the indoctrinating message. We should seek out diversity of thought, not to drink the Kool-Aid, but to grow and strengthen ourselves.

We should be taught how to think. Not what to think, anything less is indoctrination.

Offense is the new King. Treat others with honor. That says something about you. Your character matters. Speak the truth, speak it respectfully, defend the other's right to disagree, and defend those willing to be challenged. Victimhood is not honorable, jealousy is not a virtue, and celebrating toxic behavior is harmful.

The plow sits in the field. Who will pull it?

CHAPTER IV.

The Choice Now Before Us.

Families have become shattered at the expense of political ideology. People have proudly posted social media messages that state they will not tolerate those with differing opinions. We lose internal peace when we allow our feelings to be dysregulated due to the tyranny of the algorithm. The scroll becomes gospel when we can look outside and see it is not true. There is no real threat until we allow ourselves to be manipulated into doing things that are not our values.

Fights or avoiding family due to politics? Yelling and cheering someone being doxed for their beliefs, cheering others being cancelled if it is the other side? Being fired for thoughts? Do we really, on either side, want to encourage this destruction of society for a feeling? You are not a victim because of your feelings. You are allowed to have them. They are yours.

Dox the ICE agent? Assault the cop? That is not protest, it is an assault on the plow. A nation has rules we all agreed upon. It is the government's job to enforce the rules. Enter the US legally, follow the law, or challenge the lawmaker, not the worker. Want open borders? Vote. Want charity? Give your own coin. When we demand others pay, financially, or through blood, sweat, and tears, while cheering the fist. It is not honor. It is cowardice in saint's clothing.

No matter how strong your feelings are, that strength of feeling does not make it right or accurate. Sometimes our feelings lie to us. We cannot, and should not, encourage and reward adult tantrums. We need the adult to return to the room.

Celebrating protests and violence on campus because viewpoints are being expressed? Silence by professors and students who choose to suppress their thoughts and beliefs out of fear? Fear of the mob, fear of harm, fear of losing a grade due to someone being offended? This happens on campus. It should not, and all of us should not tolerate this.

It has become socially fashionable to label everything institutional racism, to find harm around every corner, and to make victims out of everyone. The truth is, no matter who we are, where we grow up, whether we come from means and privilege, or from poverty, life is unfair.

That does not mean it is institutionalized; it is not a conspiracy. It is truth. In a free society, as the founders intended, we all have a chance at a better life, as long as we have freedom of opportunity. You were never promised a silver spoon, just the opportunity to get one. The founders just offered you a ladder and the opportunity to climb it. Not all the privileged live a privileged life, and not all who were disadvantaged live a disadvantaged life. However, all who learn helplessness live helplessly, at least until they learn to help themselves. This is through discipline, grit, determination, help from family, community, and through learning.

Learned helplessness is the only oppressor that never fails.

Not every abuse creates trauma, not every good thing creates positive outcomes. It is what we take from it that matters. It is true that there has been harm done to people in the name of America. It is also true that America has tried to rectify those wrongs. We should demand that this continues to happen. A bad thing that happens is not always trauma. Trauma is involuntary, but healing is not. We can heal, we should heal. What we should not do is cling to harm that did not happen to us. We should not buy the pain of the past from the pain merchants. They are selling victimhood in order to suppress and oppress in the name of helping. A trauma therapist does not tell their clients to go live in the trauma, to embrace it, to sell it, or to want to be a victim. They try to empower the individual to heal, to become better and stronger, to address what happened, and to move forward. We can, we should do this as a nation. No good therapist tells the client to hang onto the trauma forever. That is toxic. That is emotional oppression.

Are we so out of touch with reality that we take seriously those who state there is something inherently wrong with this country? That we need socialism, that we make up fascism, that we blame all sides as a threat to democracy?

Imagine if you had a pet cat, and every day, you hope with all of your might that that cat becomes a dog. That you despise that cat, yet tell everyone who will listen that you actually love it, you just love it if it were something completely different, a dog. Some treat America like a cat we insist is a dog. Love thy cat, or admit you want a leash. As the cat starves, the nation bleeds.

Honesty in loving this country, like the cat, allows for the truth to be told. That America is not perfect, that it can be better, but also that it has done better, has improved opportunities for all. People are still flooding this country because of the opportunities and freedom. Yet some want to turn it into the countries they are fleeing. All for what, because it sounds and feels good. That is intellectual dishonest.

The plow sits in the field. Who will pull it?

CHAPTER V.

Americans Already Pulling the Plow.

Collectively, we face a choice: Live our values, or pretend we do through performative acts. Give charity or force it through taxation. Even if you believe some taxation for a safety net is appropriate and just, there is a fine line where coercion replaces compassion- and we crossed that line long ago. Accept responsibility or blame others. Individually, these choices may seem small; however, collectively, they are the determining factors on whether we heal or continue to fracture.

Do we want a monoculture, where one side is defeated? Or do we want to have the cultural compromise, to work together, and to allow differing opinions? It should not be unity through diversity; it should be unity through adversity.

Organic differences in background, experience, and thought- real diversity, can and does strengthen us when it goes through shared purpose and merit. Forced diversity is corrosive, as the highest goal always corrodes purpose and merit. The founders did not promise diversity of outcome; they promised we would have a shot based on our individual merits. Suggesting some groups cannot meet standards without lowering them is the real bigotry. That myth was debunked a long time ago and should not be forgotten. Lowering standards for anyone is condescending and corrosive. The civil rights giants had never asked for the lowering of the bar; they demanded a seat at the table, the chance to hurdle the bar the same as everyone else. Pretending some groups need easier hurdles is soft bigotry of low expectations – it hurts the very people it claims to help. That is a choice. We should celebrate differences when they strengthen us, not as a substitute for competence. The choice is, how do we celebrate differences in order to work together to create a better society.

The Declaration of Independence, dated July 4th, 1776, the founders declared a truth we still claim: all men are created equal, endowed by their creator with unalienable rights to life, liberty, and the pursuit of happiness – and that governments exist only by the consent of the governed.

The United States of America, as it stands, does not need to be abolished. This country, flaws and all, still offers what much of the world lacks: the chance to rise, to work through effort, not that is guaranteed, but the genuine opportunity it provides. That is not to say that some are not harmed, that some are less fortunate, and that some do not enjoy the same silver spoon as others. It is to say that we have a choice, in a country that allows any one of us to get up, to work, to make something of themselves, is a wonderful place to be. We do not live in an ideal world; we live in a world that is, to make it the world we want it to be.

The Declaration of Independence stated governments derive their powers "from the consent of the governed." The choice is to give consent, not blame others, and act like we have not all inadvertently given consent to the current state of government. Though if we do not give consent to what they are doing, the choice is to hold the elected officials accountable, vote them out regardless of party, and demand they govern with said consent.

It should be noted that, government cannot manufacture virtue.

The choice, the most important choice, however, is an individual one. The choice is to govern oneself. Demand of yourself that which you have abdicated through a vote and want for government mandate, to act in the manner you want the government to force others into. Choose self-control, choose charity, choose environmental responsibility, choose to learn from those different from you, choose accountability, choose to help, choose to support, not condemn, choose to understand, not fear.

Take up the plow by joining the military; if not able, choose to support those who do. Not by just mere words, or just on Veterans Day. Support them in their time of need, through actions, and through respect.

Choose to start a community garden. Choose to plant a fruit-bearing tree, one that is free to the community. Choose to help others, not just demand it be done by force.

Another example of taking up the plow is the Little Free Library program. It is where communities have book-sharing boxes, where people can donate books. Individuals can then take them to read for free. Imagine that, free books, and a reduction in landfill space. A win for all.

Taking up the plow is the individual who plants extra in the garden to bring to the less fortunate, those who cannot get out easily, or to those who may be in immediate need due to a trying circumstance. My father did this when I was a child. Not expecting anything in return, just knew what it was like to be in need.

Taking up the plow is teaching our kids charity. I know a family who had their children participate in helping other children at Christmas by buying them gifts to have under the Christmas tree.

Taking up the plow is volunteering to coach youth sports, not necessarily to win, but to teach them how to compete, how to believe in themselves, how to work as a team, and how to support one another. Failure is not failure until one gives up. Failure is just a lesson waiting to be learned.

Taking up the plow is the local football team (or any other team) volunteering in the community to visit the elderly, to help with lawn care and landscaping, or just spending time with those who do not get much company. It is reconnecting the community, all ages, to build a sense of togetherness and belonging.

Taking up the plow is the ex-convict barber who mentors others in trouble with the law, helping reduce recidivism.

Taking up the plow is the local business, family, or community that plants a fruit tree for all to eat from and nourish themselves.

Taking up the plow is teaching your children financial responsibility and the dignity of earned success, not voting for loan forgiveness at the expense of others' hard work.

Taking up the plow is the individual who starts a small business, trains and employs others, and creates opportunities for their fellow citizens.

Taking up the plow is not buying that next electronic and doing something about the environment, not just demanding the government regulate it. Taking up the plow is not performative; it is action. Don't demand that others be environmentally friendly; do it yourself. Believe in solar, become a consumer of it, don't demand the government do it. Solar fields on farmland, fenced off? That is not environmentally friendly; it is just performative, not in my back yard behavior. I do not begrudge the owner of farmland making a profit off the land in this manner. However, giant solar farms that sterilize thousands of acres of good cropland while the homeowners or city folk who demanded them refuse a single panel on their own roofs. That is not just, just performative. Corporate welfare and crony subsidies are also forced charity; it is just a different recipient.

These actions are neither the actions of the left nor the right. They are actions of a citizen governing themselves. It requires no mandate, no permission, no legislation. It only requires one to govern themselves rather than waiting to be governed. The plow sits in the field waiting to be pulled. Will you pull it, or wait for someone else to do it?
The plow sits in the field. Who will pull it?

The republic is not dying.

It is waiting.

CHAPTER 6

Your Move

The republic has waited long enough.

Your move.

You have long known what the problem is. You know. You blame the other side; they blame you. It is deeper than that. You blame the politicians, yet keep electing them. You blame the system, but feed it with every single click, every share, and every performative act, no matter how deeply you feel it. It feels good, but it changes nothing.

It is the algorithm that has helped make you believe your neighbor is your enemy. Yet, daily, or almost daily, you sit by, work by, drive by, are served by, serve, and communicate with those you believe are the enemy, told to you by the algorithm. It grows when you engage. Every time you engage the rage bait, the race bait, the othering, and every time you share that thing you feel strongly about that does those very things. Choosing comfort through tribal certainty over the discomfort of self-examination. You pull the plow of the algorithm, not your own.

You are not the victim of the system; you are its architect. That means you can destroy it.

Now, this is not a policy suggestion, but it is a thought exercise. Imagine if all major institutions, such as the Senate, or Supreme Court, or even your local school board, were split evenly between perspectives you support and perspectives you oppose. This would theoretically require genuine compromise. How does that make you feel? What thoughts come to mind? If that bothers you, good. Sit with it. What are you afraid would happen? I posit that the fear or feeling uncomfortable reveals something important about whether you actually trust the founding principles of self-governance, or whether you trust only when your side is in control.

Do you trust the plow?

Here is what you have forgotten: The principled conservative and the classic liberal are not enemies. They share common and foundational values. That includes individual dignity, skepticism of centralized power, self-governance, and equality of opportunity. They have been turned against themselves by forces that profit from the division.

The neighbor who votes differently from you wants their kid to succeed, just as you do. They want to live in safe communities, just as you do; they want meaningful work, just as you do, and they want to build something that lasts, just as you do.

They may have been convinced that the only way to succeed is to defeat you.

That is wrong. So are you.

The path runs through the plow; both are refusing to pull. Why won't they pull it? Because pulling the plow means something that neither side wants to hear, you're both wrong about the other. The way forward, the only way forward, is to own all of it.

Self-governance requires us to own our successes and our failures - both individually and as a nation. When things go well, we can't credit only our side. When things go poorly, we can't blame only the other side. If we own it all – own the harvest, own the plow, our contributions and our failures - we have a chance. If we externalize the crop, we starve in our own dirt.

If we don't choose differently, if we externalize the blame and perform instead of acting, the fracturing continues. Families stay broken over the political divide, and communities continue to be divided. The algorithm, those in power get richer and stronger. And we become what we say we fear: a people incapable of governing themselves, waiting for this thing to come save us.

It is not coming; we are already here.

If enough of us choose the plow, as some already have, to govern ourselves, to own our contributions and our failures, to see our neighbors as allies instead of enemies, we don't need saving. We do not need a perfect president, or a righteous Supreme Court, or a savior from either party. We just need us, the citizens.

You have every right to stay miserable.

You have every right to succeed.

The choice is yours- and yours alone.

In 1776, Thomas Paine called on his generation to gain independence from a foreign king. On July 4th, 2026, the United States of America will turn 250. This is a call for independence from an internal threat to our democracy. From the algorithm, comfortable lies, and from tribal loyalty.

Common Sense sparked a revolution because it put a name to something everyone already knew but would not, or could not say.

The plow sits in the field. Who will pull it?

The Plow Dare List

Delete one rage app.

Listen to the other side, really listen.

Invite one conversation with someone you may not agree with

Donate time and talent, donate financially, not for feedback or praise, for the meaning of it.

Plant a little extra in the garden, plant a fruit tree to help others eat healthier.

Defend someone you may not agree with.

Listen to the full story, stop repeating false narratives on either side.

Stop minimizing real violence and exaggerating rhetorical violence.

Worry about yourself and do not try to force your beliefs or charity onto others because they may have more than you. Jealousy is not a virtue.

Give back to the community in the best way you know how.

Understand we all want the same thing.

Coach, mentor, or teach someone a skill.

Attend a local government meeting and actually participate.

Read one book that challenges your political assumptions.

Pass this on, gift a copy to someone, buy it for someone who needs a challenge.

You say you want your side to win
so the country can be saved.

Tell me again how the country gets
saved when half of its citizens
become your enemy the day you do.

You know the truth.

You have known it the
whole time.

The plow awaits.

Pull it.

APPENDIX:

Some brief remarks on the Government of the Passions.

We are not beholden to our feelings. We can choose to be mad for free, and we can choose to be mad on purpose.

This means we can have any feeling, free from consequence of harm to ourselves or others. We choose to be mad on purpose, to take control of our feelings without acting out.

I choose to be mad on purpose. That one word, "purpose", puts you back in charge of the plow.

I can choose to feel this now.

I can stay mad and still talk with others.

I can stay mad and still listen.

I can choose to not let it own me. I can pull the plow in my own life and not let the new tyranny win. I do not have to give into the othering, the radicalization at the hands of the system.

Replace the word "mad" with any emotion.

I can be offended for free, I can be offended on purpose to choose how I act, in control, within my values.

I can be afraid for free, I can be afraid on purpose to do something about it in a healthy way.

I can be righteous for free, I can be righteous on purpose to stay in control, within my values.

The second you admit this, that you are in control of your emotions, then your feelings no longer have power over you.

You are no longer at the algorithms mercy, and you become the adult in the room again.

Do you trust the plow?

www.ingramcontent.com/pod-product-compliance
Lightning Source LLC
Chambersburg PA
CBHW060531280326
41933CB00014B/3139